I0420699

THE TRUTH ABOUT EVERY-THING

TONY CARAVAN

Copyright © 2015 by Tony Caravan

Original artwork, photos, typography and design by Tony Caravan

Music performance rights through BMI.

Cover artwork by Tony Caravan

All Rights Reserved.

ISBN-13: 978-1519552662

ISBN-10: 1519552661

First Edition

ROCKFLUX : Filmworks : Music : Publishing — Rockflux.com

FORWORD

The things that people believe...

Recently I conducted a small-scale social experiment on YouTube®. The idea came to me after I happened upon a video claiming that the Earth was actually flat; and that NASA, the world governments, the media (and I guess everyone else) were all involved in one of the greatest cover-up conspiracies of all-time. And, as I perused several more similar videos, I discovered that some of them were getting views in the hundreds of thousands—which is no small potatoes.

My first reaction was that it had to be a practical joke, or one of those things that bored academics come up with as a mental exercise—like that idea that we are all part of an elaborate computer simulation. Unfortunately, this was not the case. It soon became clear that the promoters of this "theory" were not highly educated individuals; in fact, it was obvious that most of their followers had very little knowledge of rudimentary geography, math and science.

Some of the anti-globe arguments they put forth had to do with: not being able to see the curvature of the Earth; that people should be able to feel the 1000 miles per hour rotation speed; and that there was nothing beyond Antarctica—particularly the South Pole—and it was a restricted area and "no-fly zone."

So basically, I set out to address these issues, one by one, in a non-threatening way, to see what kind of response I would get. The result was far beyond my expectations.

First, without intending to insult your intelligence, let me quickly review the proof I put forward: Regarding the curvature of the Earth, I explained that there are satellite images of the planet that clearly show that the Earth is indeed round. Next, I demonstrated that the perceived speed of rotation was closer to that of an hour hand on an analog clock, since when you divide the 24,000 mile circumference by 1000 miles per hour you get 24 hours, and subsequently, day and night. Last, I provided photos and video of expeditions to Antarctica that I was involved with, showing that it actually is a continent at the bottom of our spherical world.

Here is a sampling of some of the comments that I received:

"Unbelievable. Simple again brandished a satellite image—and the Earth is round again. So, after the illusion with all these space traveling... does not work with me anymore. The earth might as well be a piece of cake—before I trust even a single image from any 'satellite'."

"Like the LIVE moon landing on TV in 1969?"

"Have we had any independent inquiry for these so called transanartic flights? Why not? Are you afraid it might prove the earth is not what you been told? Lets have you pay a few flat earthers and independent trackers to fly from South America to South Africa or Austrila or new Zealand. What are you afraid?"

"Cognitive dissonance will make YOU believe that there is nothing wrong... You will tell yourself that the world has gone mad and we are a bunch of nutters! Rather than realising that you are indeed suffering with Cognitive dissonance. WAKE UP!"

"So Antartica exists...we already knew that. You got to go to your Government approved location (no doubt closely watched) and you saw some snow, whoopee. You've now concluded that the Earth is not flat coz you saw Antartica. I better forget all about the Earth being flat and go back to the spinning spaceball whizzing around the sun coz YOU saw Antartica...lol"

"Our Earth Is a Flat Motionless Plane. Break through the cognitive dissonance so you don't end up becoming one of the last fools to wake up. Stop tying to cling on to the Globe. It will be History! time is running out for the Globe. how can you ignore nearly a thousand facts? WAKE UP. It's not even funny anymore how fast asleep some people are."

"The stars are just little lamps to fool us. The Sun and the Moon aren't real."

"...a perfect example of what to many vaccinations can do to a mind. His unthoughtful and unintelligent comments reflect the sheep that he has become."

"The problems in the world are caused by the same people who make us believe in a wrong earth."

I guess my favorites are the people who actually used the term Cognitive Dissonance[1]. Without realizing it, they are actually describing themselves. The rest of the comments were just too bizarre or profane to waste time listing or discussing here; though I did respond to many of the them, only to receive the kind of comebacks you'd expect from a three or four-year old child.

---

1 Festinger, L. (1957). A Theory of Cognitive Dissonance. California: Stanford University Press. "The idea that when conflict arises in one's belief system, the resulting tension must be eliminated. People will find some rationale for whatever is causing the conflict, or they may choose to ignore the event in question altogether." —Leon Festinger

This experiment exemplifies the gullibility of humans to believe practically anything if it is presented to them in a manner consistent with advertising or public relations techniques. And, once convinced, how they will hold on to those beliefs tooth and nail to the end. It's an unintended side effect (if you will) of years of conditioning by the education system, preachers, media and politicians. Furthermore, the extent to which these beliefs proliferate over social media, demonstrates the power (and control) in the hands of those who know how to utilize the various platforms of information dissemination.

Now I reckon my assessment might also be considered somewhat of a "fringe" statement; and, as far as the so called "mainstream" is concerned, it is. Which leads us to a dilemma in modern society: If the truth (and its supporting arguments) can be dismissed as lies and heresy; and, on the other hand, fantasy can be believed as fact—all depending on the order and/or presentation of the material—we have entered into a very dangerous period in human history.

What good is a global mass communications network and instantaneous access to information, if the truth can be manipulated or discredited? And how can we expect to advance as a people, if we have an education system and media that create false realities for millions of people for socio-economic-political goals?

Of course there have always been individuals, institutions and governments that have successfully swayed public opinion to one side or the other. And there have been horrifically dangerous propagandists like the Nazis; however, never before in the history of the world has it been so easy to spread false information to such a large global audience.

The reason there is corruption in government and Wall Street; and the reason people turn a blind eye to our crumbling infrastructure, climate change, social injustice, the broken health care system, wage-slavery, exorbitant student loans, racism, endless wars and all of the rest; is because they are being bombarded with blather and diversion paid for by the special interests that don't want the people to see what's really going on. Likewise, there are cranks out there that have people believing the most incredible things for mercenary or insane reasons, or to just to mess with people's heads for fun.

This book is a journey for the truth, through essays, lyrics, quotations, and such the like.

Tony Caravan, December 2015

for those managing to hold on to their humanity

CONTENTS

HOW WE GOT INTO THE PICKLE WE'RE IN

So many movies and so many TV shows to watch...

Pop culture abounds! There is so much good music to listen to, and great concerts and sporting events to watch or attend. We now have WiFi enabled high-tech cars, home media centers we can talk to, and over a million apps on smartphones for practically anything imaginable. We can take our media with us, and talk and text and tweet from anywhere in the world. These truly are the golden years for entertainment—*with more than we can consume in our lifetime.*

Let's also not forget that there are still backyard decks and barbecues, swimming pools, vacations at beach resorts, amusement parks, after-work happy hours, holiday parties, workouts at the gym, dog parks, museums, galleries, sightseeing and festivals—so many fun things to do—*if only we had a little more time...?*

Then, of course, there's work. We have to pay for those cars, bars and toys somehow; so we spend the better part of the week performing tasks for a paycheck. We earn wages that are never enough to pay all of the bills, or buy all of the things we want. So we charge a little and borrow some more, and get deeper in debt with the hope that we'll eventually be able to pay off those loans, so we can do the things we really want to do, and acquire even more stuff.

Aside: That's pretty much what the government does every day.

This is why people don't pay attention to social injustice, climate change, the casualties and costs of endless wars, corporate crimes, greed capitalism, lying politicians, inadequate health care, stagnant wages, inequality, homelessness and all the rest—*who has the time?!*

Actually there are people who spend hours each day watching newscasts and reading blogs and newspapers. They're called "news junkies," and they have opinions on everything—which they tweet and post about hourly. Unfortunately, it's to an audience of other news-junkies who either: "like," thumb down, retweet or comment. And in the end, there's an awful lot of back and forth, but no issues are ever resolved and the overall state of affairs is not improved.

We live in the age of diversion. A time when humans have achieved unparalleled advancements in agriculture, communications, infrastructure, travel, science, medicine, entertainment and exploration. While at the same time, more humans are sick, hungry, homeless, uneducated, and dying in war zones, than ever before in history—*I'm talking about billions[1]*.

And yes, there are the tireless activists and protesters, and truly heroic journalists working for independent media, who are doing their very best to inform and wake people up. But too often their words either fall on deaf ears; or, like the old saying goes, they end up "preaching to the choir."

Meanwhile the corporate-backed politicians keep waging wars and whittling away at our rights and freedoms. Most of the time it's either spun as something good for the people; or not even covered, or under-reported by the mainstream media.

That's how we got where we are. And no politician is going change the way things are with a speech or the stroke of a pen.

Unless masses of people take some time off from indulging in the seductive diversions of life, and join a movement, or call their representatives in Washington, and/or support a cause by getting directly involved; all of those things that make us human will be lost in the coming years.

We are clearly heading toward a society of pacified workers who don't care how much evil is done in their names, in order for them to have what they have; just as long as they can continue to maintain their self-centered, happy-go-lucky lifestyles.

---

1 Nearly 1/2 of the world's population — more than 3 billion people — live on less than $2.50 a day. More than 1.3 billion live in extreme poverty — less than $1.25 a day. 1 billion children worldwide are living in poverty. According to UNICEF, 22,000 children die each day due to poverty.

WE LIVE IN THE AGE
OF DIVERSION. A TIME
WHEN HUMANS HAVE
ACHIEVED UNPARALLELED
ADVANCEMENTS
IN AGRICULTURE,
COMMUNICATIONS,
INFRASTRUCTURE,
TRAVEL, SCIENCE, MEDICINE
AND EXPLORATION.

WHILE AT THE SAME TIME,
MORE HUMANS ARE SICK,
HUNGRY, HOMELESS,
UNEDUCATED, AND DYING
IN WAR ZONES, THAN
EVER BEFORE IN HISTORY

DEALING WITH THE DOMINANT SOCIETY IN AMERICA

It's the 99 Percent that are the Obstacle to Change.

The most frustrating thing about being a freethinker, is finding out that you are in the minority. Our consumerism society discourages thinking too much about anything; since if you did, you might change your mind about an impulse buy, or supporting a detrimental public policy.

Most people these days are so diverted from reality that they're still living in the 20th Century—*I'm serious about that*. Apart from the high-tech devices we carry around with us, most people live in older houses or apartment buildings, with old furniture, they drive on old roads and bridges, and have mindsets in the 1980s or 90s. Even our music, TV shows and movies are comprised of samples, covers, re-makes, sequels and "re-imaginings."

There is, however, a segment of the population, the one percent, that do live in the present; and who benefit from all of the modern advances in science, medicine, architecture and engineering. And, yes, there is a spillover for those who also try to live a futuristic lush life by getting into debt and/or working most of their waking hours to afford the lifestyle and things that come natural for the rich folk.

It is the wannabes that comprise the dominant society in the U.S. They want to live like the people in the movies, TV shows and magazines. They believe the hogwash about how "in the future" technology will solve every problem from hunger and disease to climate change and violence.

What a crock! We've been hearing about the future (that never came) forever. It's a means of manipulation used by the people in power to keep the masses soothed while suffering and slaving to support the upper class. It's no different than religions promising a better life after an earthly life of abstinence and servitude. *Newsflash...* Life doesn't have to be a living hell, it can be nice for everyone, if people would open their eyes (and minds) to the truth.

Tony Caravan 17

It's not the one percent that are the major obstacle to a better life for the 99 percent; it's the dominant society (within the 99 percent)—the happy, mindless individuals who simply don't care, or who are diverted from knowing the truth, through misinformation and pop culture; or, who simply refuse to accept the truth (cognitive dissonance). And unless/until the majority of the 99 percent demand the changes necessary to improve the society as a whole, the status quo will be maintained, and the one percent will get away with whatever they want to.

Making the world a better place to live for the majority of people is within the grasp of 21st Century knowledge and technology. We just have to have the will to do it; and find better ways to communicate this to the dominant society. Clearly, the single most effective way to do this is through pop culture—the national obsession. We need more artists (of all mediums) to speak through their work; instead of going for the easy money gained by following the corporate formula for fame and fortune.

Furthermore, we need to lose the phrase "we are the 99 percent;" because it's very deceptive and simply untrue. For it is *they* who are selfishly keeping us down and living in the past; and who will ultimately lead us back into the dark ages.

IT'S NOT THE ONE PERCENT THAT ARE THE MAJOR OBSTACLE TO A BETTER LIFE FOR THE 99 PERCENT; IT'S THE DOMINANT SOCIETY (WITHIN THE 99 PERCENT) WHO FAIL TO ACT.

WHY THE ODDS ARE THAT THE FUTURE WILL BE MORE LIKE DYSTOPIA

RATHER THAN A HIGH-TECH UTOPIA

Throughout the ages people have dreamed of a better future. Whether it was a belief in an afterlife paradise, or the hope for a day when there would be an end to the daily struggle to keep their families safe—or to just to stay alive.

So many promises have been made by our so-called leaders over the millennia... Promises of peace and plenty, happiness and enlightenment, liberty and justice for all...

But just look around... How many people out of the seven billion inhabitants of this planet have achieved those things, or are likely to benefit from advances in science, medicine or technology?

The vast majority of people still struggle to survive. They work day in, day out just to pay their bills. It's called "the cost of living." *Wow!*

Then there are the talking heads on TV... They promise cures for diseases, "smart" homes and appliances, peace and security, robots to do the grunt work, better this, and better that—all coming soon. *Rubbish!*

All of those things have already happened, just not for the average person. And many more fantastic things will come along; but again, not for the average person.

Each year it becomes more and more costly to maintain a 21st Century existence. By which I mean, to participate in the culture and afford all of the services and gadgetry that define modern life. I'm talking here about the lifestyles depicted in the movies, on TV and in the magazines.

We've become addicted to consumerism; and the corporations are like drug dealers—they keep raising the prices year after year. Oddly enough, it's starting to get to the point where only real drug dealers, crooks and thugs can afford the things we've all come accustomed to.

Yeah, I know it's complicated. And most people prefer to ignore looking at the big picture in perspective to their life and their future. They see themselves getting by (for now) and figure, life's okay and it will improve in the years ahead.—*Nothing could be farther from the truth.*

The wealthy have segregated themselves from the rest of society. Eventually, they'll have very little interaction with people outside of their class. Prices for real estate, food, technology and medicine will continue to rise, until they will become totally out of the reach of the average person (even with loans and credit cards).

The very things that now pacify the masses, will eventually become too costly to afford and maintain. And, at that point (which is not too far away), we will see dystopia.

There are all sorts of possible scenarios on how exactly, when and where, it will begin for the majority of people. But it's already begun for many millions of Americans in the inner cities and forgotten rural towns across this country. Most are unaware of how bad life is for those people, since the media pays very little attention to what's going on outside of their insulated world. But for those who live "out there," life has become a surrealistic nightmare.

I don't want to say that there is no hope at all, because there are one of two things that can be done to save this country from a dystopian future:

Option One—We keep the current corporate-consumer plutocracy in place, but give every American an annual stipend to keep them above the poverty level; and/or to be able to afford 21st Century life. This would mean printing up currency (like the Fed does for the banks) and issuing it to everyone. Since this currency is only paper anyway; and, since our entire economy is based on this "fiat currency," nothing would really change (despite what the economists might say). However, this option would require strict controls on corporations to prevent further destruction of the environment, abuse of the tax code, and mistreatment of their employees. But let's face it, that's not very realistic!

Option Two—*The more realistic solution.* The U.S. becomes more of a social-democracy. Here we would keep everything the same as it is, but break up the "too big to fail" banks and make sure that the big corporations paid their fair share of taxes and operated by same set of rules that small businesses do. We would then guarantee everyone affordable housing, free healthcare and enough to eat. And yes, of course our Constitution and representative form of government would remain totally intact; but we would have to pass laws to prevent the greed-capitalists from regaining a stranglehold again—like the one that's destroying this country now.

I know there are tens of millions of people who go crazy at the notion of any kind of social program for this or social program for that; but those who do, lack compassion, and they don't see how badly the system is broken. They also don't understand that this is the only thing that can save this country from total collapse.

But let's not lose sight that any improvements to the financial system, and the government, would be an exercise in futility; unless, at the same time, we address climate change, pollution, infrastructure issues, violence and endless wars.

What good is having a roof over your head, a decent-paying job, and all of the modern conveniences, if there's rampant crime, no clean water to drink (or fresh air to breath), and a planet on the brink of World War III and self-annihilation?!

EVERYTHING YOU KNOW IS WRONG!

Most people don't want to accept that there are people with tremendous influence in this country that are so filled with hate and greed that they craft and support legislation and candidates that don't really care if the majority of Americans live in squalor and disease due to poverty and neglect.

The reason why most people don't see this, is because those rotten, selfish individuals, politicians and talking heads on the media seem to be "nice people" with "family values" who love their children. —Hell, I hate to say it, but Hitler smiled, loved his girlfriend, liked kids and collected art; but he was a genocidal mass-murdering maniac and a fascist dictator!

People in this country have to move beyond the cult of personality and realize that many of the beautiful (and not so beautiful) people in power are evil, corrupt monsters who are only looking out for themselves (and their families) and couldn't care less about the majority of people who co-occupy this country.

We already have many of the components in government that the Nazis used to expand their empire and hold on to their power.

Wake up! The American Dream is being put out like a lit cigarette on your arm. There will be no Cinderella story for you (unless you win the lottery)—and then the government will take half of that.

We need to have a Great American Tweet Out or Face-Off (Facebook off) day. Spend a couple of days or a week without diversions, and catch up on what's really going on around you; and all that has changed drastically while your head's been tilted down at your smartphone. And definitely don't watch CNN, FOX, MSNBC, ABC, CBS, NBC, PBS or read the major newspapers. Explore alternative press and news outlets/programs like RT, SkyNews, BBCWorld, Free Speech TV and Democracy Now. You won't believe how insane things have become. In fact, I'm sure it won't be long until you'll discover that…

EVERYTHING YOU (THINK YOU) KNOW IS WRONG!

ARE PEOPLE REALLY LIVING LONGER?

Back in the 1960s and '70s people only went to the doctor when they were really sick (I mean *really* sick). Many of the home remedies left over from the "old countries" were still widely used. Everything from the well-known chicken soup therapy and mustard plasters to vaporizers and "feeding a cold and starving a fever."

The thing is, these things actually worked. Case in point, my grandparents made it to their 80s and beyond without taking a bunch of prescription drugs or regularly visiting a doctor. And most of my friends all had older grandparents as well.

This anecdotal evidence seems to contradict many medical journal articles and mortality statistics. *Why is that?*

Simply put, it's not life expectancy that has increased, it's the manner in which the mortality rate is measured, along with the advent of "life support" technologies that create the illusion that things have improved.

The CDC[1] lists the current death rate in the U.S. as 821 per 100,000 people (or 2,596,993) per year; with the average life expectancy being 78.8 years.

Statistically, way back in 1970 it was 70.8 years; meaning that, by the numbers, we've gained of a whopping eight years over the last 45 years. Now granted, for a person 70 years old, that sounds like a reprieve of eight more years. However, for a nearly comatose person in a nursing home with feeding tubes, oxygen, bed pans and/or a daily regimen of prescription drugs in between mealtimes in a semi-private room and having to be bed-ridden for the rest of their life; it's more of a benefit for the family that won't let go, than a decent quality of life for the inmate.

But let's sidetrack for a moment to the causes of death in the recent past... Nearly 60,000 U.S. soldiers were killed in the Vietnam War and over a half million lost their lives in WWI and WWII—

---

1 Center for Disease Control Deaths and Mortality cdc.gov/nchs/fastats/deaths.htm

nearly a million were wounded. Disease outbreaks in the early part of the 20th Century took millions of lives. Not to mention all of the industrial and automobile accidents that occurred until safety regulations were passed. All of this lowered mortality rates.

In the post industrial revolution and war eras, air pollution (smog) was rampant in the major population centers, and the use of poisons and carcinogens like asbestos and lead in paint and gasoline were ubiquitous. Processed foods were also gaining market share.

In spite of all of that (at least up to the 1960s), the American diet was still fairly healthy; with fresh fruits and vegetables available in almost every neighborhood. Plus, most people knew how to cook; and certainly the pace of life was a lot slower. There was less stress.

From 1970 to today, the U.S. population increased by over 100 million people (100,000,000). And as would be expected, demands on resources and infrastructure grew tremendously during this time period. There were more mouths to feed, more bodies to house, more waste to dispose of, and eventually more people on Social Security, Medicare, disability, unemployment, etc.

All of this was more than the government could handle or afford; especially with corporate tax rates down and industrial production (and jobs) leaving the country.

Enter the privatization of America... If the government could no longer guarantee "life, liberty and the pursuit of happiness," private corporations could—for a price.

Everything from ginormous medical institutions to big pharma to nursing homes and health insurance conglomerates to local water and sewer authorities to private prisons, military contractors, etc.

Big chain "box" stores replaced the neighborhood fresh food stores. Industrial farms replaced the small independent farmer—you know the rest...

Basically, the U.S. government became corporatized and the price of everything went up. It now took two members of a household to work to pay the bills (and taxes). Suddenly everyone was working longer and harder with less free time to enjoy life. We were less like human beings and more like cogs in a machine—wage slaves.

We became dependent on processed "junk" foods since there was no time to cook after work; and weekends were the time to catch up on the household chores. America became unhealthy and obese, despite the fact that we were more productive and spent more time working.

Now over 600,000 people die each year from heart disease, and over a half million die of cancer. There's Alzheimer's, strokes, diabetes, and respiratory diseases. Not to mention that, so called, "accidents" still kill over 130,000 people a year.

The statistical life expectancy may have increased to justify pushing back the retirement age (for Social Security payments); but the quality of life expectancy has gone way down.

Some people may live longer in "managed care facilities" and by taking countless pills and having frequent doctor visits, tests and annual hospital admissions; but what kind of life is that?

The elderly are either warehoused in cold institutions, or stuck at home popping pills and watching television all day long. Even the healthier ones can't go out for a walk to the corner grocery store or social club—they don't exist anymore! That and the fact that most of our streets are no longer safe for pedestrians.

No, as far as I'm concerned, the mortality rate has gone down in the last 50 years—that is, mortality for being human.

We're losing our humanity, but most people are too side-tracked and diverted from reality to see it.

ODD THINGS PEOPLE DO WITHOUT THINKING ABOUT

PARTIAL LIST:

1 **Working out at a gym instead of being able to get normal exercise walking or doing things outside.** The fact that people accept that they either have to work too long (inside), or that it's not safe to be outside in most places is completely unacceptable. Artificial workouts are unnatural.

Following that line of thought...

2 **The whole concept of working during the best hours of the day, and for most of the week (and your life), just to pay bills.** This is an amazing feat of indoctrination from pre-school through to your first job. And it completely goes against all logic of being human. The idea that we have to work at meaningless tasks to support a select few (one percent); and all that we get in return are a few hours of leisure time a week, and barely enough money to survive, is slavery. But we're too brainwashed to see it; and the sad part is, most people have become content doing this.

3 **The obsession some people have with country and patriotism.** The country in which you are reading this right now is just the spot on the planet where you are currently living. It's understandable that people like their home or form of government; but it's still just a physical place and ideology, respectively. Being proud of your country is like being proud of a pile of rocks—they're just pieces of the Earth and nothing more. Besides, we all know that pride always leads to prejudice.

4 **The worship of leaders and the cult of personality.** The so called "people in charge" are just your representatives. In a democracy, by following them, you are technically following yourself. No person living or dead is any more special than you are. It's nice to respect people, appreciate wisdom; but hero worship and admiration of the superficial elements of an individual is not just absurd, it's wrong!

Which brings us to...

5 **Saluting and singing to flags.** They are just banners—pieces of cloth with colors and symbols on them. The idea of getting bent out of shape over a woven piece of cotton or polyester is truly mass insanity.

6 **Fighting, killing and hating to make the world a better place.** Peace will never be achieved through violence. Deep down inside any compassionate person knows this to be true. The justification of murder for the acquisition of land, fossil fuels or to change a form of government is not a valid argument —it is an excuse. While defending yourself can sometimes turn violent, most people of good conscience find it abhorrent.

and,

7 **Money and credit**. Money is only made of pieces of paper or chunks of metal with numbers printed or engraved on them. Credit is a phantom ledger in the cloud. The idea that most of a person's life is spent either in the acquisition of one and the payment of the other is complete and utter madness.

All of these things and more are the influences affecting daily life, the structure of societies, elections, wars and other tragedies of modern human existence.

If you can find a moment to contemplate this, a moment of clarity, as they say, you just might wake up from the nightmare.

MONEY IS ONLY MADE OF PIECES OF PAPER OR CHUNKS OF METAL WITH NUMBERS PRINTED OR ENGRAVED ON THEM. CREDIT IS A PHANTOM LEDGER IN THE CLOUD. THE IDEA THAT MOST OF A PERSON'S LIFE IS SPENT EITHER IN THE ACQUISITION OF ONE AND THE PAYMENT OF THE OTHER IS COMPLETE AND UTTER MADNESS.

THE TRUTH ABOUT POLITICIANS, THE WORLD

ET. AL.

Most people view the world they live in from the perspective of the forces of influence in their life. By that I mean the society they were born into, how their parent(s) raised them, the curriculum of the schools they attended, their workplace, friends and acquaintances, and the information they receive through the media and pop culture.

In most instances, like here in the U.S., people are polarized between, so called, liberal and conservative group stances on what to do about crime, drugs, the military and gun control, human rights, the law, inequality, social programs, the environment, economics, politics, immigration, etc. However, very few of the positions we take on important societal issues of the day can be broken down simply by the left or right, Republican or Democrat, FOX or MSNBC, black or white, patriot or pacifist, tree hugger or polluter, gang-banger or the average person, etc.

There's a back-story and nuance to practically everything. Serious matters that affect all of our lives and future generations should require our full understanding of all aspects of the issues; and that means being able to see things in perspective and comprehend "the big picture."

In this age of sound bites, tweets, posts and photo captions, the average person makes a split second decision on which "side" they are on when they are confronted with news and information. There is an instant response to "like," "re-tweet," etc. Just like in public opinion polls, there is no attempt (or time) to view the details or context of what is being presented; just an overwhelming need to accept or reject the material before moving on to the next item.

We tend to agree or disagree, vote for or against, say yes or no, believe or don't believe, like or dislike. In most cases there is no option to "agree in part," "like it a little bit" or "disagree with the entire premise."

A perfect example of this bipolar division is the two party political system in America. Despite the fact that there are other political parties in the U.S., the only news coverage is for the Democrats and Republicans. And even within those two parties, there is little primary coverage of candidates that present ideas that are not in line with the established party platform. Subsequently, many people end up voting for the "lesser of two evils" instead of a candidate that represents their actual viewpoints. Elections are won this way.

This is why things have gotten progressively worse in the U.S. despite the fact that there have been both Democrats and Republicans in office on and off for the last several decades.

I shouldn't have to elaborate on how violent crimes and shootings have become commonplace over the past few years, or how there are conflicts erupting all over the planet. Or how the financial and commodity markets are in turmoil, or that our total disregard for the environment is causing water shortages, deaths and disease.

There is a worldwide refugee and migration problem of people from third world and exploited countries trying to escape to Europe and America. And while we should do all we can to help these victims of oppression, conflicts and poverty; ultimately, the demands they put on the economies of the countries they enter, may not be sustainable.

This is a perfect example of an issue that can't be viewed as being "pro or against" immigration reform; rather, we need to look at the causalities of why people are fleeing in droves from their native lands, and deal with the long term effects and strain on the countries they migrate to. It's a very, very complicated issue.

Likewise, inequality in America has reached levels not seen since Medieval times. The burden of debt and taxes that the average person must carry throughout their lives to just have a roof over their head, eat to survive and hold down a job is becoming unbearable.

And despite all of these realities, politicians are making feel good stump speeches that basically say, "vote for me and I'll set you free." Nothing is further from the truth. For example, Hillary Clinton is backed by some of the most powerful bankers and corporations, but she purports to be a candidate for the people. She also pretends to be a progressive, but is pro-war and against universal healthcare. Likewise, Republican hopefuls are offering to "take the country back" in an appeal to the average "middle-American." But everything they do will benefit the people at the top and further sink the average Republican into debt and cause them to struggle to survive.

And I know everyone has arguments to defend their leaders; but that's the problem. They look to these candidates as "leaders" instead of mere representatives of the people. In a democracy, the power is supposed to be in the hands of the people who send surrogates to Washington to do their bidding. But we've lost that. This is the age of the cult of personality. People want someone dynamic and strong to be "in charge" and take care of them; while, at the same time, they're also supposed to solve all of the problems of the world and generally just make everything okay.

Good luck with that. It's time to wake up and realize we are teetering on the edge of collapse. If the institutional media (all of them) don't start looking beyond the status quo and write and report stuff like this, you can look forward to dystopia in as short as a decade or two—scratch that—perhaps much sooner than that.

Remember, solutions come from informed individuals; and right now, the majority of people haven't a clue as to what's really going on, or the consequences of their inaction.

THE PENDING ECONOMIC CRASH

A WORSE CASE SCENARIO

I hope I'm wrong, but there are a number of indicators pointing that things may be starting to unwind.

Most economist know that the U.S. stock market is being falsely propped up by the government and financial institutions to maintain the status quo. Ordinarily this would just be considered business as usual on Wall Street, and wouldn't really matter very much to the average citizen. But whereas the U.S. economy is based on debt (bonds) and paper money (fiat currency); and foreign countries like China (who own the bonds and trade in our dollars), are selling those bonds, we could see another crash soon. Couple that with the credit crisis, and the inability of The Fed to stimulate the "real" economy with low interest rates, it's not a question of "if," rather <u>when</u>.

The short term fixes which have given traders a false sense of security; and have encouraged them to buy further into the market, won't last very long. And, ultimately, when the debts are called, it will be discovered that there are trillions of dollars in shortfalls. To solve this problem there will be a rise in interest rates and perhaps a combination of deflation and hyper-inflation. This will put further strain on consumers (you and I) and cause the collapse.

The low price of oil has also been used to keep inflation down—and it has worked pretty well; however this will no longer be enough to prop up the U.S. dollar. *Let's just hope they don't raise our taxes!*

When you consider that millions of people are barely getting by right now; all it will take is a little nudge in the wrong direction to cause mass financial suffering. And, considering how unhinged people seem to be lately, it could get pretty crazy out there.

There's no need to worry (just yet). It's a big country and the unraveling won't happen everywhere at once. In fact, some areas and people will be less affected. However, it would probably be prudent to make sure you are not too financially exposed; and have some "physical" hard currency like gold or silver. *Good luck!*

THE NEW NORMAL

Every now and then I question my sanity when it comes to the way I view the current state of being, here and around the world. It is clear that my gut feelings are diametrically opposed to those of (what appears to be) the majority of people.

Looking around I see a culture of violence everywhere. From the speeches of politicians and subsequent actions of our military, to the story lines of movies, TV shows and games. In most instances the heroes have guns, and their followers and fans wallow in the glory of the violence and destruction that they reign on others. The justification for violence is always the same: complicated geo-political-corporate interests or simply to protect the homeland. In most cases (like in recent years), the major accomplishment of these real world military campaigns is the death and dismemberment of soldiers and civilians, and the total annihilation of cities and other cultures. While millions have been killed, injured and displaced over the last decade or so, nothing has improved; in fact, things seem to keep getting worse everywhere.

Here at home we are seeing unparalleled violence and almost weekly mass shootings. It's as if there's some sort of brain disease going around that encourages people to kill others and/or themselves. It's really gotten out of control...

Meanwhile most people are struggling to pay their bills. We work too hard and too long just to be able to keep a roof over our heads, clothes on our bodies and have transportation to and fro our jobs. People are stressed out, unhealthy and reliant on drugs or escapism to divert them from reality.

The cult of personality has become the new popular religion. People worship the warriors and powerful and the rich and famous. The accumulation of wealth and material possessions is the primary goal of most people.

The U.S. as a "melting pot" of varying races, creeds and cultures has only half-worked. There are still many people fighting integration. And rather than just "live and let live," they perpetrate hate crimes against each other.

We're also short-sighted—afraid to look ahead. Probably because unconsciously we know we're destroying any chance for a better future.

So there you have it... I guess the new normal is war, violence, hate, wage-slavery, debt and materialism. People just avoiding reality by keeping their heads buried in their smartphones until it's time for their number to come up.

What a waste...

IN MOST INSTANCES THE HEROES HAVE GUNS, AND THEIR FOLLOWERS AND FANS WALLOW IN THE GLORY OF THE VIOLENCE AND DESTRUCTION THAT THEY REIGN ON OTHERS.

THE JUSTIFICATION FOR VIOLENCE IS ALWAYS THE SAME: COMPLICATED GEO-POLITICAL-CORPORATE INTERESTS OR SIMPLY TO PROTECT THE HOMELAND.

HOW DIFFERENT ARE WE?

I recall hearing or reading something years ago that there used to be only a couple dozen different car keys; and that your key could open the doors of many other vehicles of the same year and model. However, the odds of your finding a match was pretty low, due to the laws of probability. I don't know if that was an urban legend or not, but it illustrates what I'm about to discuss very well.

We like to think that we are all unique. That out of this planet's seven billion people (7,000,000,000), and the 100+ billion of people who lived and died before us, that there is no one individual exactly like us.

Think about that... Out of billions and billions of human beings, we are different than all of the rest. Different body structures? No, not really, Hollywood uses body doubles all of the time. And anyone who has frequented a public beach or swimming pool has surely seen, or even mistaken someone for, another person who looks exactly like someone they know. So, technically, a lot of us have the same body build, size, color, hair, complexion, etc...

What about physical capabilities? We've probably all seen someone on the street, or at the gym, that walks, runs or exercises like someone we know. And certainly those who follow sports, have seen athletes who perform just like others. So when it comes to how our bodies work physically, many of us are very similar.

In medicine, human studies are conducted on a regular basis on everything from blood chemistry to organ function, and in these studies, people are often grouped into categories based on their similarities, susceptibility to diseases, and responses to external stimuli and/or drugs being tested, etc... So internally, many of us function the very same way.

Which basically leaves us with our brains, personalities, or our souls (if you will)... First off, we now know that the human brain itself, as an organ, grows, functions and responds the same way in most of us—the differences being in its size, relative health and how it is structured that determines our intelligence. Therefore, the physical brain does not make us distinct. Where our uniqueness comes in, is in what we call our personality; and beyond that, what religions refer to as the spiritual aspect of existence. Out of respect for all religions and philosophers and theologians, I won't get into a discussion of the metaphysical here (see page 55).

There is no doubt that you are different than your neighbor and the people you work with, even those people on the streets, in buildings and at the parks. It's even safe to say that among tens of thousands of other human beings, there is no one exactly like you. But the question is, how high does that number go? 50,000? 100,000? Perhaps even a million or two?

Once you start talking about tens of millions of people, the possibility of your being truly unique diminishes. And, with the societal pressures that encourage uniformity on everything from entertainment and fashion to beliefs and politics; the odds of your body type and personality matching someone else's who has a similar personality increases.

I know there are all sorts of arguments that can be made on everything I've discussed here. But considering that we are all made from the same "stuff," and that most of what we see in nature follows a pattern and obeys the (known) laws of physics; you have to at least allow for the possibility that there may well be several (if not many more) copies of you walking around, and/or who have lived on this planet in the past.

No matter what you take a way from this, when you take into account that most people eat the same foods, wear the same clothes, watch the same shows, etc., one thing that's undeniable is that we are all becoming more and more alike.

And, however humans originally came into being, there is no doubt in my mind that we are bio-engineered machines. Whether you believe in a metaphysical creator, or in the desire of the cosmos to become aware of itself; or some random spark in a primordial soup; our existence does seems to serve a purpose. And for me, that purpose is surely not to spend most of our lives working meaningless jobs to buy meaningless products and to keep ourselves diverted from reality, and to be distant and apart from nature.

If we continue on this path of uniformity and conformity, then we will have failed as a species. And, actually, come to think about it, we probably already have.

THE TRUTH

INSTEAD OF WORRYING ABOUT COMPUTERS, ROBOTS OR NANOBOTS TAKING OVER THE WORLD, WE SHOULD FOCUS MORE ON HOW THE BIOLOGICAL MACHINES [WE HUMANS] ARE RUNNING AMOK AND RAISING HAVOC ALL OVER THE PLANET.

THE FUTURE IS ABOUT SERVITUDE TO OUR CORPORATE FINANCIAL SLAVE-MASTERS

"...unceasingly we are bombarded with pseudo-realities manufactured by very sophisticated people using very sophisticated electronic mechanisms. I do not distrust their motives; I distrust their power." —Philip K. Dick, 1972

It's both amazing and depressing to discover how little the average person knows about the extent of corporate-financial influence on elections; and ultimately, the laws that are passed, and how the government is run on a daily basis. Even most of those who work within the system—the bureaucrats, the media, and order-takers—are unaware of who is pulling the strings of the elected politicians and for what goals.

Simply put, we are being ruled by an elite class that taxes us and over-charges us for the essentials of life. Their goal is more power, more property, more resources and more money. In previous centuries it was called slavery and feudalism. And while our "cages" may have become more comfortable (for the moment), we are nonetheless living in a prison.

It's not these "rulers" who are enslaving us that are the biggest problem, it's the blind followers and order-takers that are allowing all of the injustices to occur. And as I said before, forget about the one percent; the real culprits are the majority of the 99 percent who are sitting by idle, and diverted from reality, while all of our rights and freedoms are being stripped away.

We're being betrayed by people who will end up suffering the same fate as all of us—a future of servitude to the corporate-financial slave-masters.

ON SELF-DRIVING CARS

"Mickey Mouse popped out of my mind onto a drawing pad 20 years ago on a train ride from Manhattan to Hollywood at a time when business fortunes of my brother Roy and myself were at lowest ebb and disaster seemed right around the corner." —Walt Disney

This whole self-driving car craze is nuts*!* Why not just improve mass transportation? If personal privacy is a factor, bring back the old "state rooms;" or, for longer trips, innovate the "car train" idea, where you can more easily drive your car on and off at more stops.

Whether cars are electric or not, there are too many of them to begin with. It could be way faster and way better to take a "bullet" train from Philly to Boston or LA to Vegas (if they'd improve the routes, the trains and the passenger experience). And, it would be a helluvalot cheaper to do the latter than build millions of new cars.

Of course, we all know the reason they want to do this. A car is a disposable appliance—a very expensive one at that. And the thought of being able to sell millions of $30K+ appliances every five years or so is music to the ears of the greed-capitalists and financiers.

We're so far behind the other advanced nations in transportation and infrastructure that it's pathetic. In Europe you can hop a train and be in another country, in the center of town, in no time. In Japan, you can be in the next city, in comfort, in two shakes.

Enough with the planned obsolescence already; and enough with trying to re-invent the wheel and build better mouse traps. Let's see some real innovation. How about a paradigm shift, or just some better trains?*!*

THE TRUTH ABOUT REALITY

PROLOGUE

It is unacceptable that we don't have the answers to certain questions; and it boggles my mind how the vast majority of people ignore these, so called, mysteries of life.

Civilizations come and go. It's been this way for thousands of years—maybe even much longer. When you consider that the Earth is over 4.5 billion years old; it's not hard to fathom that somewhere over that deep time, a brief epoch of say a few hundred thousand years transpired, where other sentient beings could have existed, but got lost in the archaeological record. Particularly when you take into account giant impacts and other natural disasters that may have terraformed the surface of the planet numerous times. Obviously, after any of these events, all evidence of previous advanced societies would vanish without a trace—after all, even styrofoam and nuclear waste eventually disintegrate.

Think about it, the oldest records on Earth (that we are aware of) are etched in stone; but when rock turns to magma—even they will be erased.

Then again, perhaps our ancestors adapted to living in the sea—the aquatic ape hypothesis[1]—and survived deep under water during violent upheavals.

Considering the brevity of our current human existence, one would think that there would be more of a focus on enlightenment than self-centeredness. But the behavior of homo sapiens seems to lead to a repetitive cycle of discovery, advancement then greed, followed by diversion, ignorance and self-destruction.

But I reckon it's not all our fault. Genetics also plays a big part. Like seedlings that grow into predictable flora, and eventually a forest or jungle; so DNA may pre-determine the precise physical and social outcomes for humanity.

Biology, chemistry, physics and mathematics hold the answers to all of the eternal questions. Understanding this reality is the

---

1 Observation that some traits that set humans apart from other primates have parallels with aquatic mammals, or that humans may have had ancestors more aquatic than previously imagined.

challenge of the 21st Century intelligentsia. Being human is the new underground religion, and creative minds its prophets.

But why care? Does anything really matter? If everything we build and create is ultimately destroyed, why bother contemplating, discovering or creating? Why push the brain beyond the pursuit of food, sex and shelter?

What else is there? Love, social networking, spirituality and an afterlife? Man-machine interface, astral projection or some other ultimate detachment from the body? Don't forget, you'll probably need a power source to keep your synaptic-soul alive and connect with the Great Cosmic Consciousness[2]. Better figure out how to tap into (and ride) the Universal Wavelengths[3] before you keel over.

Maybe all of the sciences and religions are simply diversions from a cold, hard reality—one that our primitive brains will never come close to comprehending. Then again, our whole existence may be a computer simulation, or a dream state; or, maybe the known universe is really just a 'micro-verse' in a petri dish; or worse, the patriarchal religions may be true, and we're like pets, and we'll have to bow down and worship some dictatorial deity for all eternity to stay warm and fed.

Considering that we may be standing on the precipice of human extinction. I believe it's worth exploring what we are, where we are, and why we are.

---

2 Belief that the universe is an interconnected network of individual consciousnesses, connected to every other one.

3 String theory postulates that quantum particles vibrate at certain frequencies in and out of multi-verses throughout the continuum similar to music in harmonic relationships. Also see Theory of Everything.

THE TRUTH

CONSIDERING THE BREVITY OF HUMAN EXISTENCE, ONE WOULD THINK THAT THERE WOULD BE MORE OF A FOCUS ON ENLIGHTENMENT THAN SELF-CENTEREDNESS.

BUT THE BEHAVIOR OF HOMO SAPIENS SEEMS TO LEAD TO A REPETITIVE CYCLE OF DISCOVERY, ADVANCEMENT THEN GREED, FOLLOWED BY DIVERSION, IGNORANCE AND SELF-DESTRUCTION.

RULERS AND LEADERS

What a pathetic civilization this Fourth Age[1] has given birth to. A pre-occupation with self-centered trivial pursuits; and an evolutionary dead end brought on by deadbeat predators. What a blight on the living Earth modern humans are. Not that previous generations have done any better. History and archeology are full of the tales of rise and falls. What really gets my goat is that I came into being during this one.

There's nothing worse than beings of limited mental capacity behaving as if they are intelligent. I'm talking about the so-called rulers and leaders scattered across this planet. The self-proclaimed nobility who draw lines on the continents to divide and conquer. Those who have achieved wealth and power by killing, destroying, pillaging and enslaving. Kings, presidents, dictators, clerics and CEOs who have molded the world into their private playground and rigged marketplace.

But what's worse than these laughable-elitists, are their idiotic followers and worshipers. The race of videots[2] caught up in the cult of personality: Spectators and consumers, mercenaries, order-takers and the faithful.

Our society is decaying from an overdose of sitcoms, reality shows, b-movies, nightly newscasts, sporting events, computer games and social networking. Reality is fading into dreamtime in front of a flashing rectangle on the wall or in our hand. Nearly everything we do, eat, drink, wear, drive, talk about and believe has some root influence from a talking head or post on a plasma screen or LED display.

We're losing our ability to feel and interact as flesh and blood beings. We're becoming a race of sub-humans—programmed as perfect consumers and a slave race to serve a perverse aristocracy. All for what? To be able to download files, own a smartphone and post hourly activities? What's really bizarre about this whole muddle is that this global obsession—the center of everyone's life—didn't even exist much more than a decade ago.

---

1 According to the Mayans, we are now living in the Fourth Age which was reset in 2012.
2 Term coined by Tony Caravan many years ago and derived from the obvious: video idiot.

GODS AND RELIGIONS

Religions primarily serve as a psychological conditioning model of the hierarchy of power. There is the god-king (patriarch), followed by his angels and disciples (members of court, politicians and public servants); and of course, the saints and sinners—the obedient subservients pitted against the non-believers (creative-types and non-conformists).

The flock of followers are kept in line through a system of fear and reward. Historically, there has been much to fear. From the Crusades[1] and The Inquisition[2] to the Conquistadors[3] and colonialism, people the world over have been tortured, raped, slaughtered and enslaved—their land and resources stolen—all in the name of religion. On the other hand, the rewards of "conversion" have to be taken solely on faith—the belief in something that cannot be proven.

Obviously, all religions are complete and utter nonsense. They are childhood fantasies—fairy tales for adults—organized by those who have come to rule and prosper from the misfortune of others. They deal with an age old problem of the evil kings and robber-barons: how to enslave large numbers of people and lessen the possibility of a revolt. The solution was an imaginary afterlife and all-seeing eye in the sky. No matter how miserable your life was—working and paying taxes to the land-grabbers and warriors—you would eventually be happy living in the clouds after you die. And if you disobeyed the tyrant's rules, you would be damned to burn in a Dante-esque imaginary hell-inferno.

Of course, anyone who has flown in an airplane knows that there's no heaven in the water vapor above us. But still many still believe their bodies will be "swept away." Where? Perhaps to a planet, a spaceship or comet? Of course, little thought is given to the "faithful" who died in the past, their bodies long decayed, with only a soul that survived.

---

1 By many accounts over 1.5 million people were killed in the religious Middle Age Crusades.
2 Over a 100,000 people were investigated and tortured with as many as 5,000 people being killed as a result of the Spanish and Medieval Inquisitions.
3 It is estimated that as many as 15 million native Americans were killed by the Conquistadors with another 40 million dying from European diseases.

There is no sight without eyes, no music to hear without ears, no conversations without mouths, no lovely scents to smell without noses, no soft embraces or pain without hands and skin, no sex without genitals, and no contemplation without brains... At best, the gods were/are, by definition, extraterrestrials; or at worse a fabrication by those that who rule through deceit and manipulation.

It's really sad how the concept of religion has been transformed from a means of passing down morals and spiritual advice into a method of control, money-raising, a justification for wars and killing, and a platform for extremists.

The so-called rulers and leaders are simply the managers put in charge of the real estate by those who claim to be the property owners of the Earth—the rich and powerful who scooped up all the best land throughout history. The real absurdity here is that, these murderers and thugs, have many people convinced that a god has ordained them as the caretakers of the land; and we all must pay them taxes, rents, maintenance and/or interest to live on the planet we were born on—just as they were.

I realize that some of these ideas can be difficult to accept, especially since the lies of our rulers have been so methodically ingrained into all of our collective psyches since childhood— over generations. But the truth is, we don't have to be followers or slaves—all living beings have an equal right to the land and resources of this planet. *Why wouldn't we?*

Of course none of this really matters, since there is nothing that can be done about it. The rulers have become so powerful, that they are god-like in their ability to see all, control all and unleash their wrath upon us.

Humans appear to have a genetic defect that encourages them to admire their oppressors—kind of like the Stockholm syndrome[4].

Future generations will have the last laugh. Since civilizations are so fleeting; everything we do, and our leaders build, will fade, decay or be destroyed. Eventually, mankind is bound to get it right— one would think.

Homo sapiens are the only animals (that we know of) that are cognizant of their mortality. And certainly no good has come of this awareness. Organized religions and governments have been trying to divert us from this line of thinking for millennia. And while

4 Psychological phenomenon whereby hostages express empathy and sympathy and have positive feelings toward their captors.

some of us are immune to the their brainwashing; nonetheless, the inability of most people to find peace and acceptance in living a full (though finite) life, has created a lot of stress and depression; and good business for the psychiatrists and pharmaceutical companies.

Perhaps the disconnect between the perception of mortality and not wanting to die, or see others around us die; is wired into our brains to spur us on to find a solution to this dilemma.

Maybe we actually are immortal, but for some reason the genes that renew our cells are turned off or got damaged somewhere down the line. I know there is an incredible amount of research in the area of life extension—both through biology as well as technology—but I fear they're probably missing the point to it all.

The more spiritual religions teach us that there is a vibratory path of "oneness" and "connectivity" with the Universe; and that is the ultimately the secret to eternal life.

I wonder what the last Neanderthal thought on the last day of his life.

THE SCIENTIFIC APPROACH

When you study the behavior of the smallest particles in the Universe, you realize that everything (including us) is here, there and everywhere—simultaneously. The concept of space-time becomes blurred, and reality is only a perception. *Who are you? Where are you? What are you?*

If our brains rely solely on our senses for self-awareness and the perception of the space around us (and all of the things that we encounter); how can we be sure that reality, as we perceive it, is real? Furthermore, if the existence of our bodies is subjective, then do our brains even exist?

Following this logic, does anyone else exist besides me? Are you merely part of my god-consciousness; or is this writing part of your virtual reality? Both cannot be true. It is quite possible that one of us may not exist.

On the other hand, our cognitive experience points to another possible explanation; that we are all part of a computer simulation—a very elaborate game. The beginning of the Universe can be explained by the day the game started—that's why we can't comprehend anything prior to the "big bang[1]." And infinity is simply our inability to understand the parameters of the game, and/or when the program will end. This can be quite frightening for those that have been counting on an afterlife.

There is another possibility—one closer to what the religious believe; that we are simply what we are—a biological creation. An experiment living in a petri dish—with a start date and a plastic wall around our universe. We could even be an undetected outgrowth— that may be swept out of existence when discovered during cleaning. Imagine a cosmos that is no larger than a subatomic particle.

The fact that we cannot disprove any of these possibilities is perhaps the most puzzling of all. To not know whether we are real or not, living or artificial intelligence; or, part of a micro-verse, is pretty scary stuff. But all of this is beyond our sphere of influence. And even if we were able to prove one of the above through quantum physics, it still wouldn't change our reality.

---

1 Theory that the Universe began some 13.798 billion years ago from an infinitesimal "singularity" that exploded and expanded into everything there is today.

ANCIENT VISIONS

"When human beings began to grow numerous on the earth... the LORD saw how great the wickedness of human beings was on earth, and how every desire that their heart conceived was always nothing but evil, the LORD regretted making human beings on the earth..." —THE BIBLE

Not so long ago, a bright green comet, Lulin, passed backwards towards the Sun. In ancient times, such activity in the heavens would be attributed to Hermes, the messenger of the gods, and son of Zeus and Maia (from the Pleiades). A warning perhaps; or a sign of positive (or negative) change ahead? It may seem hard to believe, but astrology, and this kind of thinking, was the predecessor to modern science.

When we consider that life develops from adaptations and changes to our DNA; and inevitability of biological outcomes, then why is it such a stretch to imagine the predictability of all things on a grand scale through the observation of the harmony and order of the Universe.

Let's say you somehow survived the last great cataclysm on Earth—the earthquakes, upheavals, great flood[1], fire and brimstone—all of that. You were from an earlier civilization which had advanced science and technology. After wondering the Earth for many years, you stumbled upon more primitive survivors. Your basic knowledge of how things work would seem god-like to these hunter-gatherers living in caves. If they didn't kill you (or eat you), they would probably worship you for (re)creating such wondrous things using only the materials at hand.

Next thought... What if Tiahuanaco[2] (Tiwanaku) and Puma Punku are remnants of the civilization before the last Earth change? The precision of engineering and lack of stone carvings could lead one to imagine modern day buildings. And if they are indeed over 17,000 years old, then the accepted history of the planet is wrong.

And what about the obsession with stars like Sirius and the

---

1 Stories and myths of a "great flood" exist in most ancient cultures that precede the most popular (and recent) Biblical flood tale of Noah's Ark.
2 Pre-Columbian city in western Bolivia of an empire that flourished prior to the Inca Empire.

Pleiades in ancient cultures. Is it because they were bright in a world without electric lights? Or is there some significance or relationship between the heavens and earth? Did the "Age of Aquarius" begin on February 14, 2009? If so, what does that really mean? And did the great galactic alignment of 2012 happen and usher in a new era?

I reckon all of this is laughable in a world where science and thinking are for the few and far in-between geeks. Most inhabitants of contemporary, "developed" nations are pre-occupied with bright and shinny objects, stage and screen performers, violent spectator sports and high-tech gadgets. It's a world where governments maintain control over their citizens and shape foreign policy through military actions, and death-diplomacy to control all the others.

Of course this creates a strong argument against the "dream within a dream" perception of reality. Unless you believe that the absolute detail in the archaeological record and physics of the Universe is all part of one helluva computer program, or a really intense dream—seems more like a nightmare.

A tree grows, our bodies grow, a river flows, so lightning goes... For some reason, it's all the same pattern.

IT'S A WORLD WHERE GOVERNMENTS MAINTAIN CONTROL OVER THEIR CITIZENS AND SHAPE FOREIGN POLICY THROUGH MILITARY ACTIONS, AND DEATH-DIPLOMACY TO CONTROL ALL THE OTHERS.

DOOM AND GLOOM

Not so long ago, Jupiter was hit by something that caused a black spot to appear in the atmosphere. As usually is the case, an amateur astronomer first discovered it.

Speaking of impact events... According to NASA, on April 13, 2029, asteroid 2004 MN4 will just miss the Earth by skimming some 18,600 miles (30,000 km) above the ground. As a reference, geosynchronous satellites orbit at 22,300 miles (36,000 km). There's a remote possibility it may hit us; or at least maybe pinball a satellite or two. Either way, this is a once in a millennia event—though actually its due to return in 2035.

POLE SHIFT, SUPER-VOLCANOES, SUPERNOVAE, et. al.

If you're not familiar with the term pole shift, it refers to a flipping of the magnetic poles (north becomes south). Most "theorists" contend that it could happen rapidly and cause great upheavals on the planet. However, though mainstream scientists agree that pole shifts have occurred in the past, they refute the claim that they could happen quickly; rather the accepted belief is that it occurs gradually over time. But interestingly, there is evidence that magnetic north has been moving considerable distances in recent years.

Subtle changes in the tilt and rotation of the Earth are also believed to have caused climate changes regularly throughout history. They may even have led to some extinctions. While the temperature of the Earth is steadily rising due to the increase in greenhouse gases, there may be colder weather in the Northeast US due to axial tilt. There is also the remote possibility that the Atlantic Conveyor Belt[1] could slow or stop, causing a mini-ice age, or at least very cold weather in the northern U.S. and Europe. This means some regions may skate right past global warming and actually cool; however, the rest of the planet won't be so lucky, unless there is a super-volcanic eruption that would block out the sun with soot and reflective sulfur particles, and negate the effects of CO^2 build up in the atmosphere.

---

1 Global ocean current conveyor belt that helps regulate climate around the North Atlantic

PARTICLE PHYSICS AND THE CULT OF PERSONALITY

According to Einstein, gravity is not a force, rather an effect that the mass of an object has on the fabric of space-time. Kind of like the weight of a bowling ball on a mattress. The problem with that explanation is that it doesn't necessarily account for the behavior of sub-atomic particles; and/or if the mattress (or Universe) is turned upside down. :-)

The more recent String Theory[1] offers a better explanation of particle physics, though oddly enough, it is more mystical than scientific. For millennia, it has been believed that "everything" operates on wavelengths and that by "tuning in" to the vibrations, it puts you at one with the Universe (om... nam myoho renge kyo). How absurd and ironic it would be, if centuries of science brought us back to the age-old metaphysical beliefs.

In any event, this brings us to diversion and the Cult of Personality[2]. As the mass media obsesses over memorials for dead people, sports scores, the right for people to own more and more guns, girls with big breasts, singers and dancers, show-offs and such-the-like; society is kept in the dark about practically all of the truths of human existence. People are taught to admire, worship and follow the very individuals who are screwing them over and destroying the Earth.

This is a sad and pathetic commentary on 21st Century life, and probably the beginning of the end for our civilization as we know it. Not that we've achieved much. Sure, we've created some nice machines, fun toys and came up with a bunch of very interesting theories (about practically everything); but in the grand scheme of things, we've done very little to improve the quality of life for most of the people living on the third planet from the Sun.

---

1 Theory that quantum particles vibrate at certain frequencies in and out of multi-verses throughout the continuum similar to music in harmonic relationships. Also see the Theory of Everything.
2 Similar to hero worship, except that it is established by mass media and propaganda.

In a world of untold wealth and advanced technologies, with genetic breakthroughs and rocket science; billions of people "lead lives of quiet desperation." We're polluting the planet, using up all of our resources, fighting territorial and commodity wars, dumbing down the masses so they will work and slave (and borrow) just to pay for land, water and food that they already have a birthright to. Most advancements in science and medicine benefit only those who can afford them, while the rest of the inhabitants work long hours just to survive.

Meanwhile people waste what little "free time" they have reading blogs, posts, tweets and editorials, watching TV reporters, listening to sound bites and debates—supporting a two-party political system, where every eight years the other party comes to power, and things get progressively worse for mostly everyone. The only people who seem to benefit from politics are the politicians, lobbyists (and their corporate sponsors), and of course the media who make out like bandits on all of the political ads.

If you really think about it, despite all of the promises by politicians over the past several decades, the quality of life for the average citizen has progressively gotten worse—even though both parties have had the chance to be in power every four to eight years.

And as for science, well, I guess the jury is still out on whether or not we'll be saved by science. But I wouldn't get my hopes up...

AS THE MASS MEDIA OBSESSES OVER MEMORIALS FOR DEAD PEOPLE, SPORTS SCORES, THE RIGHT FOR PEOPLE TO OWN MORE AND MORE GUNS, GIRLS WITH BIG BREASTS, SINGERS AND DANCERS, SHOW-OFFS AND SUCH-THE-LIKE; SOCIETY IS KEPT IN THE DARK ABOUT PRACTICALLY ALL OF THE TRUTHS OF HUMAN EXISTENCE.

PEOPLE ARE TAUGHT TO ADMIRE, WORSHIP AND FOLLOW THE VERY INDIVIDUALS WHO ARE SCREWING THEM OVER AND DESTROYING THE PLANET.

Tony Caravan

LYRICS

Gullible

by Tony Caravan (BMI)

They tell us that they bomb and kill to protect us,
and that their wars are fought for freedom;
but each year we become less safe,
and we lose more of our rights and freedom.

They tell us that their trade deals are good for us,
and that they will create more jobs;
but each year more people are out of work,
and the price of goods and services keeps going up.

They tell us that they stand for law and order,
and that justice will be served;
but each year they disregard the Constitution,
while their campaign donors and lobbyists commit crimes.

They tell us that they know what's best for the country,
and that our taxes will be put to good use;
but each year more of our infrastructure crumbles,
and the air and water is poisoned, while their salaries go up.

The tell us that this is the greatest country in the world,
and that they are doing a great job;
but each year there are more homeless, unemployed,
poor and sick citizens—all struggling to survive.

The tell us that they will improve the education system,
so that "no child will be left behind;"
but each year there are more drop-outs and illiterates,
with un-payable student loans and no jobs for their degrees.

The tell us that this is the land of opportunity,
and that the "American Dream" is alive and well;
but it's clearly only true for a select few
of TV personalities, movie stars, musicians, models and athletes;
not the hard-working majority of the American people.

The tell us to vote for them,
because they will fix all of this;
but every four or eight years a new candidate is elected,
and we work harder for less with more stress and suffering.

available on iTunes® and other online music sources

Everything's Broken

by Tony Caravan (BMI)

The bankers are all crazy
if they think people will keep paying their
student loan bills and high interest on credit cards

The politicians are all insane
if they think people will keep paying their
taxes for this, and taxes for that
with no representation just social injustice

The landlords are all living in a dream world
if they think they can keep raising the rents
and people will keep paying for boxes with doors

(chorus)
There's no going back to the way that it was
Everything's broken and can't be fixed
Half the people are delusional and
most of the rest are living in a virtual reality
The fantasy has no happy ending
Just wars and violence, destruction and hunger
until it goes back to the way it was
before the greed and hatred and vanity
to starting from scratch after Earth has its way.

Wall Street traders are idiots
if they keep playing the market like a casino
The bottom's gonna drop out and they'll
be jumping' out windows like their granddaddies did

The media are fools
if they think anyone cares about the stories
they weave and the importance they place on trivial pursuits

The warriors got played
by a weapon industry that makes money by selling
to both sides. The more chaos they create,
the more profit they make

(chorus)

continued

The corporations are mad
if they think their profits will rise
People aren't going to pay for their products
that break or out-date too soon

The government will fall
as the people ignore it and laugh at their antics
and realize they don't need them anymore

(chorus)

Nagasaki Sunrise

by Tony Caravan (BMI)

Like a Nagasaki sunrise after the bomb,
there's a haunting beauty in nature, but not in man
Evil dwells in the blackened souls
of the order-followers and bureaucrats,
and the crowds that cheer them on

But what kind of madness leaves such
death and destruction (back then and today)?

How many Nagasaki-like sunrises
must there be before the masses are awakened?

Heroes don't carry guns or kill for the suited cowards
in statehouses and corporate boardrooms;
true heroes teach, they heal, they build
they think and create and love

We've created a culture of violence
From the speeches by politicians to pop culture icons
People now wallow in the glory of destruction
and their humanity has been traded for paper money
and objects of diversion and justification

Though "with all its sham, drudgery and broken dreams,
it (still) can be a beautiful world"
But first we must take the first step
back towards being human (and away from violence)

Actually there was no beauty in the Nagasaki sunrise,
after the bomb, and there will be no beauty
when all of (our) humanity is gone.

available on iTunes® and other online music sources

2016

by Tony Caravan (BMI)

While politicians make promises to
save or change the country
Everything's crumbling all around us
And the prices keep going up.

They all pledge to create new jobs
fixing the infrastructure;
But those aren't jobs for the
millions of unemployed.
If the work would ever materialize
it would go to the big contractors
with their heavy machinery.
Not workers with pick and shovels.

The personal debt crisis in America is
totally out of control.
We're charged monthly for services
that at best should be once a year.
The bankers pay little or no interest
but we pay double digits on credit
Another form of enslavement
like taxes and fees and adjustments.

Our news is filtered to please the
advertisers and corporate sponsors
No one knows what's really going on
except when a whistleblower comes forth
But the media is always quick to discredit them.
Meanwhile we pay for subscriptions
on media services that have commercials
They double dip us and we ask for more.

The planet's weather is all screwed up.
It's beyond the tipping point or what
reductions in emissions can solve.
Most don't know that the government
messes with the weather modification
and we know what happens when you
mess with mother nature.
Climate change is happening now
and it's only going to get much worse.

The widespread violence on the streets
keeps growing - as does the social unrest.
Already thousands of neighborhoods
across the country are unsafe - even deadly.
A warrior culture and militarized police
only exacerbate the problem
People have forgotten that peace is good thing.

The winner of the presidential election
will be the one who tells the most lies,
raises the most money, and suckers the
most people into believing they will make
everything better - like they always do.
People want to be led, to be lied to,
and told that everything will be o.k.

The truth is, 2016 is the turning point
When the Earth's climate goes beyond repair
When debts will be too high to ever pay off
When wars and violence will spread like disease
When the bridges, pipes and roads will collapse
When the cost of living becomes too high
When the lies outweigh the truth
When it becomes apparent that we are nothing
but slaves with overprices smartphones and cars.

available on iTunes® and other online music sources

THE TRUTH

Tryin' To Catch The Wind

by Tony Caravan (BMI)

There are so many things - that upset me
So very many things - that drive me mad
I don't know why - it affects me
For most people - it doesn't seem that bad

I write, I rant — every chance I can
Change the channels, read the books
Sorting fact from fiction
But everything I do…
it's like tryin'… tryin'
tryin' to catch the wind
[tryin' to catch the wind]

There's that girl - on the TV
Smiling with - political news
There's that girl - in the movies
Making people - change their views

They write, they rant - every day they can
On every channel and newsstand
Hard to tell what's fact or fiction
Finding out the truth
is like tryin' tryin'
tryin' to catch the wind
[tryin' to catch the wind]

available on iTunes® and other online music sources

TWEETS

@realTonyCaravan

Considering the short life of tweets, and how they get lost on the over-crowded scrolls on the net, I thought it worthwhile to preserve some of them here in one place, for future reading…

Injustice is everywhere, yet people either ignore it, adapt to it, or simply make it a topic of political discourse; meanwhile it worsens.

Perhaps the most serious problem facing us all is the gullibility of people. It is an unintended side effect of advertising and propaganda.

Over-prescribed (profitable) Opioid Rx drugs kill 15K/ year in U.S.; heroine overdoses are also on the rise. Both come from Afghanistan.

Fresh water shortages as climate warms; Oil prices to double by 2020—U.S. to sell reserves (HR1314); Japan in recession; Gold jumps 1%.

There's no substitute for long-form reading. Those who do, get it; those who don't fall victim to endless news & political cycles and decay.

Paradox of plutocracy: You'd think since they make trillion$ off of us, they'd at least give us Camelot, instead of acting like f'in Nazis.

The majority of people in the U.S. are either poor, underpaid (and struggling) or, getting by with tremendous debt. Yes, the majority.

Congress now says people can own resources in space. Really? Nobody owns space for cryin' out loud!

Here's a novel idea... "No taxation without representation." And since the government represents corporations, let them pay the taxes.

Focusing on a presidential messiah to fix all wrongs, only delays fixing all that's wrong for another year. Time is a luxury we don't have.

Latest gov't/Wall St. scam: worthless paper money is used to buy gold "shares" that aren't backed by gold; thus keeping gold prices down.

It's up to the 99% to stop the TPP. Like everything else, the 1% may push & sell it, but the majority of the 99% apathetically let it happen

Nearly 60% of U.S. population takes at least one prescription drug; 15% take five or more

All empires fall due to the drain on the economy by the military. The U.S. will be no exception. This should be a presidential debate issue.

It's almost laughable (but not) that when very bad things occur, politicians are quick to condemn (on camera), but do nothing to prevent.

So mass shootings are now accepted as part of our culture? Mere news items or questions for candidates? Media & politicians are jellyfish.

Money in politics is out of control... "TV spending is projected to hit $4.4 billion for the 2016 election cycle."

Wage-slaves must endure an endless cycle of bills and taxes—an obstacle to true freedom as human beings and the pursuit of happiness.

Corporate and financial influence (control) of government has reach unprecedented proportions. We're not electing reps, we're being ruled.

Stress kills. Tens of millions in the U.S. are stressed out over the cost of living and debts; while Wall St./bankers profit on the tragedy.

SocialSecurity fact: $50K/yr. salary gets you $21,672/yr. If you retire at 67 and live the avg. 78 yrs., you pay MORE IN than you get out.

The costofliving (expenses) for more than half of all U.S. workers and Social Security recipients is higher than their monthly income.

The law of cause and effect is universal. Too bad sociopaths only see the first part of the consequences of their actions and not the karma.

Gun advocate argument busted: By having guns you are protecting yourself from criminals or fascists. Fact: Both out-man you and out-gun you.

The 3 realities: 1) Where people look the other way; 2) People talk about injustice but do not act; 3) People suffer because of inaction.

They should eliminate fees for taxpayers who bailed them out; likewise, the Fed should print cash to pay our debts.

People who watch the major network/cable news programs get a version of events that's almost totally different than what's really going on.

As if the U.S. doesn't know who, what, where and when hard drugs enter. It's become key to the economy like weapons.

Rather than Columbus Day celebrating a mass murderer/thief, it should be replaced with indigenouspeoples Day to celebrate their cultures.

Our education system's primary focus is to prepare students to be obedient workers rather than free thinkers. It's a drone/slave society.

The clash of civilizations and cultures is the primary cause of wars and violence. Not everyone wants to be assimilated. Live and let live.

Too many people in the U.S. are living on the edge. Couple that with easy access to guns and a warrior culture and you get Umpqua shootings

There are over 30,000 deaths EACH YEAR in the U.S. due to motor vehicle crashes; yet auto ads keep pushing speed and tech in cars & trucks.

Everything You Know Is Wrong!

Imagine if half the resources to wage wars, elect politicians and entertain were used to improve the human condition.

"..how great the wickedness of human beings... and how every desire that their heart conceived was always nothing but evil." —Noah's Flood

Sometimes an over-simplification of the issues is what's needed. That said, the political system in the U.S. is a farce. Plain and simple.

Rights or "privileges" that governments grant you; are as absurd as rules, permits (permission) & taxes—all were created to enslave you.

Happy Peace Day! An end to all wars and violence begins with each of us - at home, in our neighborhoods, the workplace and everywhere we go.

My advice to the megalomaniacs running things... Wanna see your name up in lights? Change your name to EXIT. And make like a tree and leave!

If you think about it, it's greed, pride and selfishness that's the cause of man's inhumanity toward man. We need more love & compassion.

This year there has been (on average) the equivalent of a group or mass shooting every day in the U.S., and countless murders. No more guns!

Gun violence in the U.S. is out of control. We need a Constitutional Amendment to outlaw guns. End the wars and stop praising the military.

The human animal is ceasing to advance as a species. Our reliance on external technologies for survival is dehumanizing and de-evolving us.

The first migration is due to war and poverty; the next will be due to climate changes; the final will be to escape the horror that unfolds.

Spoilsport: I hate to report that U.S. politics, social issues and world affairs are no longer funny. While we laughed, they pillaged & won.

As wars & violence escalate everywhere, consider this: both the Democrats and Republicans have blood on their hands.

The degree of lies & propaganda spewing from corporate-controlled politicians & their media mouthpieces is so deep, it's invisible to most.

Anyone who believes that a few new laws and social reforms will make things better is living in a dream world. The entire system is broken.

The human species suffers from mass insanity. To be continued...

Man's inhumanity to man can be seen in corporate greed, endless wars, destruction of the environment, politics, and how we treat each other.

Constantly switching between American Apartheid, Presidential Politics, Hollywood, Sci-Tech & the Daily Struggle to Survive is Mind-Melting.

There is a better way... All societal problems can be solved by looking a level or two behind the surface and becoming less self-centered.

Greed & lust for short-term profits = short-sightedness when it comes to looming climate, healthcare, crime, housing, jobs & water issues

It's gotten to the point where there's practically a major tragedy every week, and daily misery for tens of millions. The system is broken.

The key to understanding socialissues, politics, life and it all is knowing that sometimes everyone is a little right and a little wrong.

Many in the media and politics seem clueless as to the magnitude of discontent in the U.S. It's not about left or right, it's about life.

The story of civil rights in this country can best be described by that Springsteen line, "ONE STEP UP AND TWO STEPS BACK."

It's a sad commentary on the state of affairs in the U.S. knowing that people actually watch CNN, FOX, ABC, NBC & CBS for news and opinion.

While other countries plan and build for sea level rise, the U.S. builds more prime real estate in flood zones like NYC and the coastlines.

By viewing people as simply consumers and cheap labor, corporations and politicians ignore the impact over-population has on the planet.

We live in a dehumanized society that focuses on gadgetry and diversion to stimulate our senses. We're slaves to corporate-politico masters.

The real reason why people are against national health care, safety net programs and immigration reform is due to their greed and prejudice.

The transfiguration of the U.S. from a democratic-republic to a plutocracy with figure head politicians is mind-boggling. Most don't see it.

Humanity only exists "in the flesh." Today most forms of social interaction are now being processed by machines.

"The Dogs of Corporate Masters" - Your tie is your leash, and your shirt collar is self-explanatory...

THE BIG PICTURE

You often hear people talk about how there's a lot of multitasking going on today by both the young and the old. The reference usually applies to their ability to navigate several apps at once; like talking on a cell phone while also texting or tweeting, or maybe even playing a game, or watching a movie. Some negative examples of this is are people who text while driving a car, or who use their smartphone or browse websites while at work. And, while switching back and forth from different activities is kind of a component of multitasking, it's not multitasking.

The word multitasking comes from computing, and refers to a processor that can execute multiple programs simultaneously. It has sometimes been applied to humans—usually geniuses—who have an uncanny ability to focus on multiple things at the same time. And while they may switch back and forth from various mental activities, they are totally cognizant of everything all at once.

Which brings us to the title of this essay, "The Big Picture."

While it is commonplace in our society to change channels, talk on the phone while doing something else, play games and text, walk and chew gum, etc. What is not as prosaic is the ability of people to focus on multiple thoughts, ideas, formulas, facts and events at the same time. In other words, to be able to see and comprehend "The Big Picture."

We tend to move from election cycle to election cycle, tragedy to tragedy, holiday to holiday, game to game, celebrity gossip to celebrity gossip, and back and forth and in-between. What we don't do, is see things the way they really are—in their entirety, and grasp how they interrelate to one another, and the causalities and consequences of our actions and inaction.

It's not because we're dumbed-down (though one could make a substantial argument for that); rather, it's due to the manner in which information is made available to us; and, subsequently, shared to the society as a whole.

The two primary causes of our inability to seize and hold on to more than one idea at the same time are advertising and public relations, or as some might say: profit and propaganda.

The major media, which are the primary source of news and information for the majority of people, is a for-profit system; whereby it is dependent on ads, commercials, subscriptions, sponsorships, etcetera to function and prosper. And, in order to maximize its revenue, it must capture and hold on to as many ears and eyeballs as possible. This usually means sensationalizing and dragging out stories in the biggest possible way for the longest amount of time. And while often times the truth can be found in paragraphs or digital clips contained withing these stories, they are usually buried beneath the juicy stuff that appeals to people's base emotions. Things like hate, anger, greed, lust and pride.

The big media companies are businesses after all. They have to turn a profit for their shareholders, and to be able to afford the salaries of the expensive talking heads and creative producers and technicians that make the news programs appealing to the masses. Of course they are going to use the time-proven techniques that the advertising and public relations industries developed into a science.

Politicians also work from the same play-book, though many times their audience is not only the public at large, but the people in the media as well. They have become experts at misdirection, bait and switch, and downright lying to the people with smiles on their faces, with their families and celebrities by their side.

What this means is that the game is rigged, and if you really want to know the truth about what's going on in this country, or around the world—past, present and future—you have to be your own investigative journalist. Which is a sorry state of affairs considering the incredibly sophisticated mass communications system that exists, and the potential it has for informing and educating the public. But unfortunately, if you want the truth, you have to go out and search for it yourself.

On page 102 I've outlined some of the topics that rise and fall from the headlines, and a few that rarely surface. Use this as a guide, and perhaps like me, you'll start to see "The Big Picture." Warning: It's not pretty, and it may cause you serious stress. *All the best!*

WE TEND TO MOVE FROM ELECTION CYCLE TO ELECTION CYCLE, TRAGEDY TO TRAGEDY, HOLIDAY TO HOLIDAY, GAME TO GAME, CELEBRITY GOSSIP TO CELEBRITY GOSSIP, AND BACK AND FORTH AND IN-BETWEEN. WHAT WE DON'T DO, IS SEE THINGS THE WAY THEY REALLY ARE.

THE BIG PICTURE...

At any given time, all of these issues (and many more) are out there in the ether—waiting to be brought into the forefront.

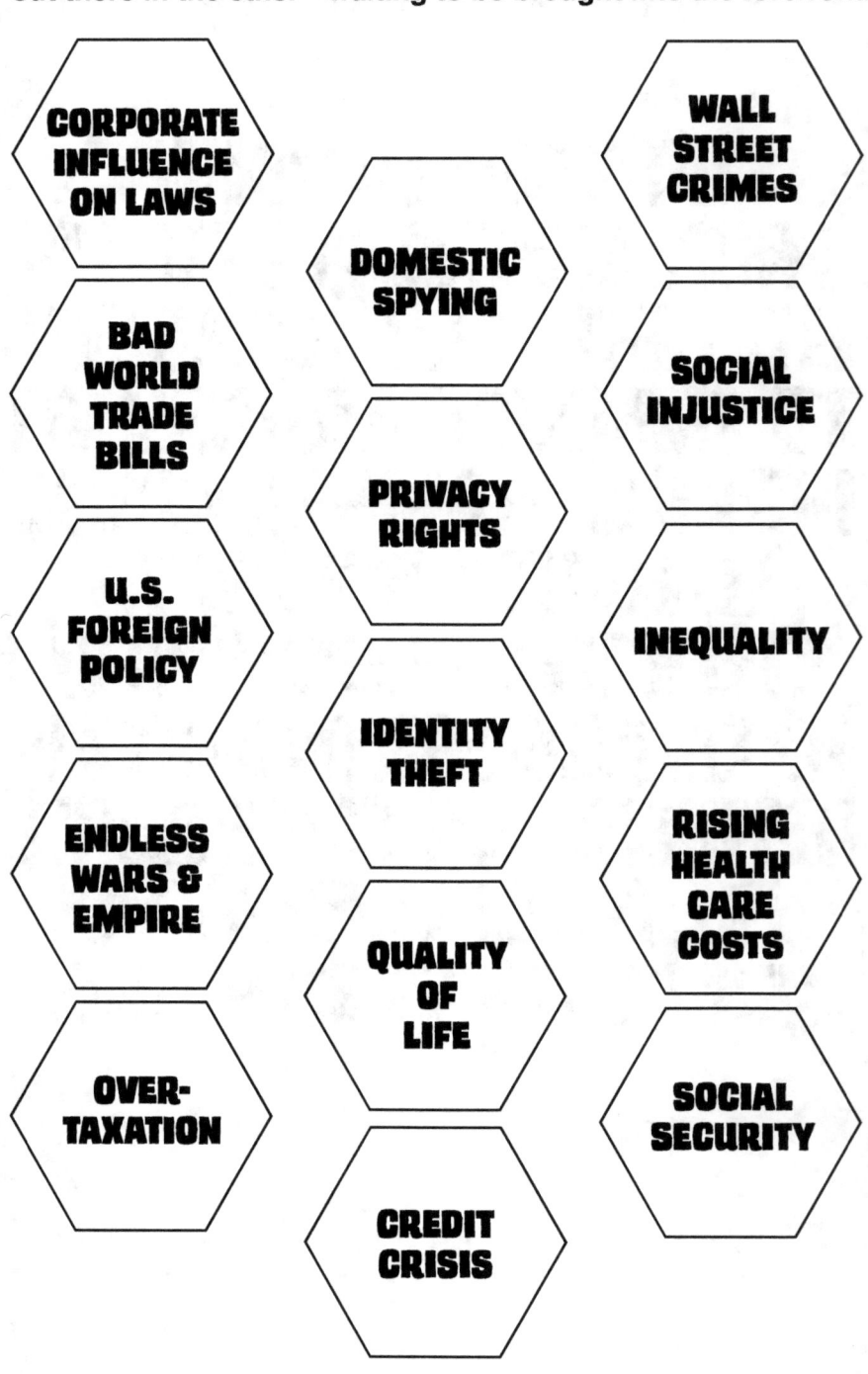

CORPORATE INFLUENCE ON LAWS

WALL STREET CRIMES

DOMESTIC SPYING

BAD WORLD TRADE BILLS

SOCIAL INJUSTICE

PRIVACY RIGHTS

U.S. FOREIGN POLICY

INEQUALITY

IDENTITY THEFT

ENDLESS WARS & EMPIRE

RISING HEALTH CARE COSTS

QUALITY OF LIFE

OVER-TAXATION

SOCIAL SECURITY

CREDIT CRISIS

THE FAILING EDUCATION SYSTEM

MILITARIZED POLICE

POVERTY & HUNGER

HIGH STUDENT LOANS

RACISM

COST OF LIVING

CRIME, GANGS & DRUGS

CRUMBLING INFRASTRUCTURE

INFLATION & DEFLATION

CLIMATE CHANGE

ISSUES OF THE DAY

GUN VIOLENCE

NATURAL DISASTERS

END OF THE OIL AGE

CLASH OF CULTURES

FRESH WATER SHORTAGES

MIDDLE EAST CONFLICTS

CULT OF PERSONALITY

self-portrait with beret, 2015

Tony Caravan is the author of several books, screenplays, countless articles and songs, and many web pages. He has worked in film, video, radio, publishing, advertising, entertainment, education and the internet.

He is semi-retired, living in a small house, in a small town with a cat, books, computers, musical instruments and a backyard garden and pond.

Inquiries and communications can be made through his website at RockFlux.com

OTHER TITLES BY THE AUTHOR...

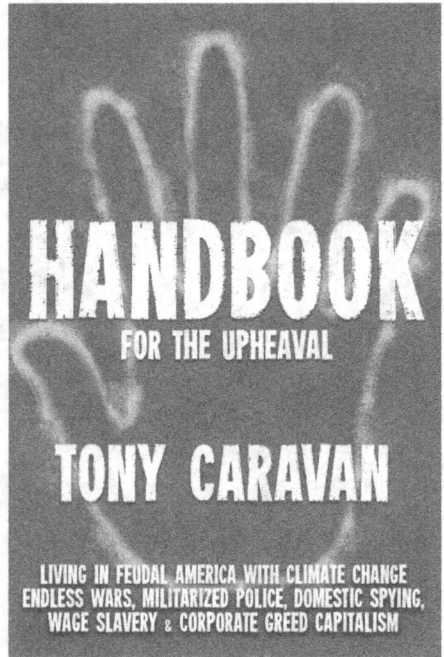

Handbook for the Upheaval

ISBN-13: 978-1514223772

available at bookstores
and online at Amazon.com

also available digitally
on the iTunes bookstore

ALL MUSIC AVAILABLE ON ITUNES®

The Non-Conformist

ISBN-13: 978-1500469498

available at bookstores
and online at Amazon.com

also available digitally
on the iTunes bookstore

The Early Years

ISBN-13: 978-1496066428

available at bookstores
and online at Amazon.com

also available digitally
on the iTunes bookstore

www.ingramcontent.com/pod-product-compliance
Lightning Source LLC
Chambersburg PA
CBHW071209280526
45787CB00002B/626